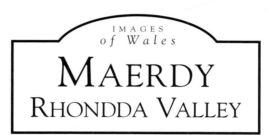

IMAGES
of Wales

MAERDY
RHONDDA VALLEY

A map of Maerdy, indicating the position of the colliery in 1979. The map was produced by the NCB to show the position of the colliery in relation to the village.

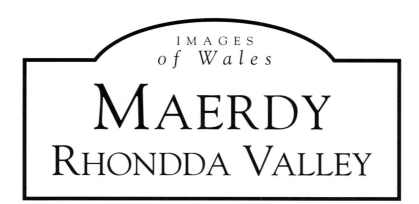

IMAGES
of Wales

MAERDY
RHONDDA VALLEY

Compiled by
David Owen

TEMPUS

Tempus Publishing Limited
The Mill, Brimscombe Port,
Stroud, Gloucestershire, GL5 2QG

ISBN 0 7524 1695 2

Typesetting and origination by
Tempus Publishing Limited
Printed in Great Britain by
Midway Clark Printing, Wiltshire

Acknowledgements

I feel very proud and privileged to have lived in Maerdy through the years that now form the memories of a generation. Thank you for all the wonderful stories and photographs of the village which have been given to me by people from the village. These have come from the first quarter of the nineteenth century through to the last year of the twentieth century.

The people of the village have been very kind; they are proud, and their community spirit will take them through the centuries ahead. Thank you to Maerdy – the most famous village in the Rhondda Valley; and the Rhondda Valley – the mast famous valley in the world. I sincerely thank everyone for their kindness and help.

The Maerdy Archive (Registered Charity No. 1073001) collect and copy photographs, plans, certificates, postcards, books and artefacts, old and new of Maerdy and the surrounding area. If you are able to assist, please contact us on 01443 732073.

Contents

Preface

The village of Mardy grew from the economic prosperity that came from the 'Black Gold' produced by the No. 1 and No. 2 Colliery. By the late 1870s the villagers had begun to hold religious services for Calvinistic Methodists and Congregationalists in the old Maerdy Farmhouse. They later left to build their own chapel leaving the Baptists to move in.

Except for the sinkers huts and a small school in 1880 the chapels were the next to be built, with Siloa in 1881, then Sion for the Baptists and Bethania for the Calvinistic Methodists in 1882. In 1885 All Saints church was built, Saint Luke's in 1888, Carmel and Weslyan in 1896, with Ebenezer opening in 1911. The Salvation Army moved from a room behind the Workmen's Hall to the Royal Cottages and other small denomination's of worship also set themselves up in the village.

In 1881 the social meeting place was the Mardy Coffee Tavern with a library and reading room. The building was paid for by a director of the colliery and in 1905 it was replaced by the Workmen's Hall and Institute. It was the largest and most central building in the community and contained numerous rooms. In the basement: Lesser Hall, classroom, billiard room, gymnasium, games room and offices. First floor: ladies' cloakroom, men's reading room, library, refreshment room and offices. Upper floor: a large hall and balcony capable of accommodating over one thousand people. The building cost nearly nine thousand pounds to build.

By this time the village had really prospered and nearly 1,000 houses had been built and the population was almost 7,000. The railway station opened for passengers in 1889 and the small group of shops of the early 1890s was later joined by a club, pubs, a doctor's surgery, chemist, jewellers, watchmaker, cobblers, newsagent and booksellers, banks, bakers, iron-mongers, fish and chip shops, Italian ice-cream vendors, confectioners and café owners, another school and the Mardy Electric Light Company. Maerdy was booming right up to the mid-1920s.

In the early days of the 1926 strike and lockout the *South Wales Daily News* ran a report under the heading 'LITTLE MOSCOW'. During these times there was the industrial depression, the 'means test', along with much hardship and suffering. Nearly every family relied on the dole as only a few were at work and this state of affairs continued up to September 1939 when the Second World War began and the 'the best coal in the world' was once again sought after.

`In 1948 the National Coal Board planned to invest £5 million to redevelop Mardy No. 3 and No. 4 Colliery. In the1950s a new primary school and new council houses were built, and 'Rock 'n' Roll was the music of the day. In the 1960s and '70s some of the older houses and chapels, except Seion, were replaced by flats and new houses, Teify House was built on the site of Ebenezer, and Carmel is now used by a double glazing manufacturer. A new comprehensive school was also built. In the 1980s a new doctor's surgery was opened. In the 1990s Mardy No. 3 and No. 4, the last colliery in the Rhondda Valley, closed; a community centre began breathing new life into the village and landscaping of No. 1 and No. 2 Colliery and its tip began. There has been a new road the railway station has been landscaped, Park View houses (a £30 million investment by Fenner) and a car component factory have also contributed to the new growth of the community. As we go into the millennium a community woodland is planned as well as a conversion of the bike shed which will become a youth centre. A new bypass is planned for the valley and Maerdy Workmen's Hall now stands on the site of the old Coffee Tavern where, in 1881, social life in the village began.

David Owen
March 1999

Foreword

Someone visited the school not so long ago and complained about the weather. It was a typical autumn to winter day in Maerdy with clouds meeting the mountain and the drizzle hanging to the river. The visitor said, 'Now I can see what Max Boyce meant in his song *Rhondda Grey*'. This hurt me somewhat for, as a visitor, he had dared criticize my Maerdy. Born and bred here and suffering only a few years away at college and in London in the '60s, I replied crossly, 'Scratch the grey surface and, as far as Maerdy people are concerned, underneath you'll find pure gold'. This is perhaps a romantic view of the village, but if you think of those you know as friends, it probably isn't far from the truth.

My memories of this village probably stem from two of its institutions – the Infant School (from which I would 'mitch' and hide in my Grandparent's pub, the Maerdy Hotel, listening to the tap-room banter) and Maerdy Junior School (where I have taught for twenty-six years, the last two as headteacher). My dad also taught there, in fact some two terms before it was officially opened in 1952. And so there has been a Blake in school for the last forty-five years!

Everyone has memories of the stories half heard as a child. Some of mine have drifted through my memory for so long that I now don't know if they are true or not. I could number among them stories about the dynamiting of rivers to catch a trout, or Fred Davies from the waterworks, or walking daily to school from the Top Res. I remember standing on the railway bridge to let the steam from the loco turn my legs to jelly, 'welly rings' on chapped, freezing legs in winter, 'Jabbas' watching us like a hawk in pictures, the vicar J.R. Davies on his bike, and watching the Infant School burn down.

Once you start, its hard to stop remembering snippets of information. I wish I had paid more attention to those who told the tales, for sadly many of them are long gone. David Owen and the members of the Maerdy Archive deserve praise for their efforts in recalling Maerdy's history.

Some people, in the dark days of the 1980s, claimed that the village would die. But we still have our mark to make in this ever-changing, ever-challenging country. Far from dying, Maerdy is alive and thriving. Long may it be, so that people like those compiling the Maerdy Archive will have many, many more memories to capture for our children's children.

Peter Blake
Headteacher at Maerdy Junior School

Introduction

I am very pleased to be asked to write the introduction to this photographic collection of Maerdy. Maerdy was home to me for the first sixteen years of my life, and remains my mother's home and that of many older members of my family. I now spend half my life in Westminster and I am grateful to have such a full and exciting career, but in quieter moments, 'hiraeth' is often not far away. At such times childhood images of Maerdy and its people often come to mind: black suits, brown pews and bright coloured hats at Sion chapel and the Gymanfa ganu. I also recall lines of bright red double-decker buses waiting to pick up hundreds of children, clutching their half crowns, for the annual trip to Barry Island. On the beach half circles of mothers and aunties are opening old biscuit boxes filled with sandwiches, hard-boiled eggs and lovely brown sausages.

I remember Uncle Sammy: small and wiry, black with coal, his ready smile, white and pink, shining through the dust. The tip behind our house to adult eyes was a scar, but to us it was a playground; its steep slopes were designed for sliding on an old cardboard or better still some oil cloth. The pond on top was a place of adventure – sailing a tin bath or sliding across in winter. Our gang crossed the river, black as Guinness, and ambushed the coal train throwing stones at the wagons and putting pennies on the tracks.

Few other small towns can boast such a proud, though short, history as Maerdy. One of my grandparents was one of the first children born into this Welsh Klondyke. The others came from three corners of Wales, Monmouth, Pembrokeshire and Caernavon. I have lived through the last third of the history of the town and in that time it has seen changes almost as profound as in the period before the First World War, when the pits were first sunk. The river no longer looks like Guinness and the tip no longer provide adventure theme parks for children. A town founded on coal is slowly building a new future.

Jon Owen Jones MP
Welsh Health Minister

One
The Early Days

O Glowr Di-Waith

Wedi bod dros ddeugain mlynedd
Ar ei orau'n gwneud ei ran
Nid oes iddo un anrhydedd,
Nac edmygedd mewn un man
Eto iaith llawer craith
Sibrwd ddefnydd cyfrol faith.

Nid oes ganddo dai na thiroedd
Na'r un eiddo mewn un banc.
Corfod iddo wario'r punnoedd
Y bu'n cynilo pan yn llanc.
Dyfnach craith wneud yn ffaith
Gam y tymor hir di-waith.

Anodd yw bod yn galonnog
Heb bunt oedd gynt ar ol
Pan mae'r mawrion cyndyn cefnog
Wedi gostwng swm y dol.
Dolur mwy na phob clwy
Gaiff wrth geisio cardod plwy.

Dweud er hynny mae'r blynyddoedd
Iddo groesi pen y bryn,
A'I fod bellach ar lechweddoedd
Sydd a'u godrau yn y glyn
Eto'r sant gwyr am dant
Gwyd ei galon ym mhob pant.

Mr T. D. Lewis Deacon
and 'Arweinyddgan'
at Ebenezer (C. M.) Chapel

This is believed to be the Maerdy cairn circle of stones. During the Bronze Age (around 500 BC), when dense forests of oak, alder and elm filled the valley, with pine and birch on the mountains, nomadic tribes built cairns on the hilltops and were responsible for the construction of the enigmatic standing stones and stone circles.

The Iron Age (sixth century BC to first century AD) saw the spread of heathlands and the formation of peat. In this period, iron gradually replaced the use of bronze for the making of weapons. Great hillforts were built, eventually to be used as defence against the threat from Rome: from the first to the fifth centuries AD the power of the Roman army was felt in lowland Wales, while the almost impregnable highlands were still controlled by native tribes.

During the Dark Ages (fifth to eleventh centuries AD) and subsequent mediaeval period our valley was sparsely populated, heavily wooded and remained so until the destruction of the forests for the coal industry in the nineteenth century.

Cairns are the most numerous of all ancient monuments. There are over 20,000 in Great Britain and the largest number are in Wales with nearly 400 in Glamorgan. The Rhondda cairns are believed to belong to the Bronze Age. Cremated remains were placed in a small coffin, called a cyst, over which was raised a circle of stones. There are three types of cairn that are found in Glamorgan: the cairn circle (a low cairn of upright stones on a small circle), the round cairn (a round or oval mound) and the ring cairn (a level space enclosed by a bank of earth and stones with an entrance through the bank).

An artist's impression of Castell Nos. Nearly 150 years ago, after the Norman's seized the lowlands of Glamorgan, the native lords still remained in control of the bleaker hill country and gave little more than the required recognition of Norman authority and overlordship. A number of small castles are an impressive example of the Welsh ability to build castles in impossible places.

When the castle was constructed, the highest rock outcrop at Castell Nos was partly surrounded by a ditch and the summit was levelled. It is impossible to be certain when it was built, but it would have been before 1242 when the Welsh ruler of this area was deprived of his lands by Earl Richard of Clare.

The natural defences of Castell Nos, rising high above Castell Nos Reservoir, have been used to advantage for centuries including, more recently, by the Home Guard in the Second World War.

Castell Nos, on the left, overlooking Castell Nos Reservoir. This rocky outcrop above the reservoir is where wheatears nested among the rocks and, below, foxes dug their earths and had their cubs in the sandy banks, black and yellow lizards ran about there and the clumps of foxgloves were busily attended by the bees. Here also were the groundnuts we used to dig for – a crunchy little nut at the end of a foot long stem, only to be chastised by the reed bunting as we disturbed its solitude. Wild ducks used to nest in among the peat bogs of Cwmdare swamp whose peaty waters trickled into the reservoir below.

Alongside the Castell Nos reservoir were the stunted growths of Bara Caws r Cwrw trees (The Hawthorn) who's leaves were supposed to taste like this – bread, cheese and beer. This is where the magpies nested, their presence revealed by a ball of sheep's wool and countless twigs snug enough among the prickly thorns of its host, the hawthorn tree. They were watched by the ever-present sandpiper and the dipping wagtail. The swoosh of the dipper as she scouted along the river for the larvae of the caddis fly.

The dipper used to nest all along the river especially under the bridges, often accompanied by the little Jenny wren who nested alongside. The waterfall above Castell Nos Reservoir was also another chosen spot for the dipper and the 'twink twink' of the wagtail, cozy underneath the old stone arched Pont Lluest Wen bridge by the Water Board Filter House.

Reg Sydenham

The Monkey's Tump. When money was scarce and cars were few, one of the pleasure of the summer holidays was to ramble on the mountain side and picnic on the 'Monkey's Tump'. I often wondered why there were no monkeys and thought that perhaps there had once been a monkey puzzle tree there.

It was many years later that I realized the 'monkeys' is a corruption of 'monks' and not monkeys at all. The word has been handed down by mouth and we always articulate in the easiest way: isn't it much easier to say 'monkeys tump' than 'monks tump'? Having solved the question of where the name came from, I was faced with another: why monks came to Monk(ey)'s Tump?.

Let us go on an armchair pilgrimage. Take your atlas and find Wales; put your finger on the Rhondda and take it straight down to the coast. There you will find Llantwit Major (Llanilltyd Fawr is its original Welsh name). There, in the sixth century, when the Anglo Saxons were pushing the Celts westward, Saint Illtyd built a monastery and gathered round him monks and scholars in a sort of early university. From there the monks travelled on foot, on horseback or by boat to Cornwall, to Ireland, to Brittany and of course throughout Wales to meet up with others and spread the Gospel.

We will take just a few examples of these journeys, those of the three saints: Illtyd, Dyfodwg, and Gwynno. Look at your map due north from Llantwit Major and you will find Llantrisant, where they journeyed together. If we follow Illtyd and Dyfodwg (who travelled on together) we come to a church in Williamstown dedicated to Illtyd and further on we arrive at Ystradyfodwg (the ford of St Dyfodwg). Until fairly recently most of the Rhondda was in the parish of Ystradyfodwg: at Ton Pentre near the river there is now a very modern church built on an ancient site called St John the Baptist. Here, no doubt, Saint Dyfodwg rested before fording the river and facing the climb up Penrhys to partake at Ffynnon Mair (Saint Mary's Well), which was famed for its medicinal qualities especially for eyes. He would have stayed at the monastic cell on Penrhys for a night or two and worshipped the wooden statue of the Virgin Mary, which was taken away and burnt in Chelsea by Thomas Cromwell at the time of the dissolution of the monasteries. The present statue is a very recent one. Dyfordwg would then have dropped down into the Rhondda Fach, ro refresh himself at the farm at the north end of Oxford Street. He then took the steep climb to rest on the 'Monkey's Tump' before dropping into Monk Street Aberdare, on through Llwydecoed (the wood of the grey monks) and so to Neath Abbey and eventually to St David's.

Revd Iris Thomas

A view of Maerdy from 'Monkeys Tump'. The journey of the last of the three, Gwynno, took him from Llantrisant through Pontypridd and along the crest of the mountain in Llanwonno, another ancient site, and then on again to the 'Monkeys Tump'. Perhaps Gwynno and Dyfodwg met on our 'Monkeys Tump' before forging on to St David's.

Many people nowadays, without knowing its history, will take their ashes, after cremation, to be scattered on the 'Monkey's Tump'. We Celts have always been and still are very responsive to nature and the numinous. This tump is no ordinary rocky outcrop. This is a place where the Saints have trod, where the saints have rested and broken bread. It is a thin place where heaven is very close to earth.

Revd Iris Thomas

Pont Lluest Wen also known as Drovers Bridge.

Pont Lluest Wen. On an early summer day around the middle of the nineteenth century a group of monks from Carmarthenshire set out on foot with their herd of cattle in search of good grazing for the summer months. Eventually they arrived two miles north of Castell Nos. They pitched camp and then made an annual pilgrimage to the spot. They realized there was an abundance of good grass on the other side of the stream, which the cattle were unable to cross because of the large stones in the bed of the stream. The monks therefore built a bridge, which is now known as Pont Lluest Wen, which means 'the bridge of the white encampment (or tents)'.

Eurwen Watkins

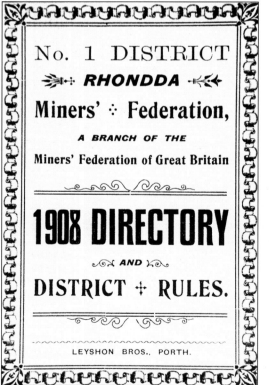

No. 1 DISTRICT

RHONDDA

Miners' Federation,

A BRANCH OF THE

Miners' Federation of Great Britain

1908 DIRECTORY

AND

DISTRICT + RULES.

LEYSHON BROS., PORTH.

A proud mother and her new foal. Maerdy derived its name from the old farmhouse, seen in the background, situated on the bank of the Rhondda Fechan River, at the northern end of the present day Oxford Street. The farmhouse was large and faced down the valley and had a large court at the front, with a high sheltering hedge. The hallway possessed a fine staircase made of solid oak. To the right of the staircase was a large room, called the parlour, capable of accommodating sixty people and to the left a large kitchen with a pantry and a dairy at the back. Neighbouring farmers and shepherds assembled here to transact important business and attend at the court of the district. The occupier of the farm was the president of the court, hence the title 'Maerdy', meaning the Stewards or Mayors House.

However, it was mining that brought prosperity to Maerdy (or Mardy as the Anglicized Coal Company spelled it).

Two

Mardy No. 1 and No. 2 Colliery

The Marquis of Bute declined the purchase of the 999-acre land and mineral rights of Maerdy Farm in 1847 and it was purchased in 1873 for £122,000 by Mordecai Jones and Wheatley Cobb of Brecon. Two years later, in 1875, Mardy No.1 pit was sunk to the Abergorki seam and a year later Mardy No. 2 was sunk. Top quality dry steam coal was produced in 1877 and then the colliery was leased to Locket and Company, in 1878, who then became Locket-Merthyr Steam Coal Company in 1879.

In 1881 Mardy No. 1 and No. 2 was the first colliery in South Wales to use electricity for pumping water. The engine, which drove the pump dynamo also drove a dynamo for lighting the pit bottoms, the underground stables and the engine houses. The No.1 up-cast shaft was 300yds deep and the No. 2 downcast shaft was 380yds deep. It was ventilated by a waddle fan and the underground working area was 2,618yds divided between east Rhondda and west Aberdare districts.

The most notable event in its history was an explosion which claimed 81 lives, although there was nearly 800 men and boys underground at the time. This tragedy, when the colliery was only ten years old happened on Wednesday the 23 December 1885 at quarter to three in the afternoon. Eighteen were killed from burns and the force of the blast and 63 by suffocation.

The explosion took place in the east Rhondda district, districts known locally as Rhondda and Aberdare. The miners in the Aberdare district were the first to be evacuated and escaped without injury. The district was gaseous, dry and very dusty and although Davey and Clanny safety lamps were used naked flame lamps were also allowed 'by permission' but evidence suggests that naked lights were used and the relighting of lamps between lamp stations were used and practised as normal routine. This practice is what is thought to have caused the explosion.

The force of the explosion blew the up-cast cage into the headgear and plunging the other cage to the bottom. The rescue team rushed to the colliery and bravely descended the pit. When they reached the air doors, lying face down was a young lad and when they moved his body they found his little dog called 'Try', his faithful friend and loving companion. The boy, David Evans of 8 Mardy Road, had tried to shield his little friend from the horrific event. The director, William Thomas 'Brynawel', was the first to descend the still smoking shaft leading the rescue team and in May 1886 he was awarded the medal for valour, for his 'coolness and devotion to humanity'.

There were thirty-eight horses underground at the time of the explosion, but only fifteen survived. There were success stories though: Jack and Jerry, two Welsh ponies, were not found until Boxing Day, and when brought together made a terrible fuss of each other; Warrior and Champion went 'neighing mad' in their stalls and had to be restrained with timber. However, there are also stories of great tragedy: fireman John Evans leading a party out of the affected area called 'fresh air, here boys' and dropped dead.

The shaft was cleared by four o'clock in the afternoon on Sunday 27 December and work resumed on Monday the 4 January 1886. The assurance companies were quick to make payments for immediate relief and also an allowance of three pounds was made for funeral expenses. Every widow received five guineas, each child under thirteen, two shillings and six pence and payments were made by noon on Christmas Eve, the day following the explosion. A relief fund was also set up by the Lord Mayor of London, Sir William Thomas Lewis.

The area where the explosion took place was at the north west tip of the Rhondda district where arching was being carried out with a hard heading being driven overhead and 'brattice' directing the flow of air. Mr Griff Thomas, the manager, gave details of the safety practices at the arching: safety lamps and a naked flame comet lamp were used. Relighting of lamps were allowed within one hundred yards of the working face and was approved by the colliery agents.

Despite such a tragedy, work continued apace in the colliery and the output of coal from No. 1 and No. 2 colliery in 1895 averaged 1,200 tons for nine hours work. The colliery, also known as Lockets', operated the mine until the general strike of 1926. Lockets' went out of business at this time and was closed. It was reopened in 1932 by Welsh Associated Collieries, who were taken over by the Powell Duffryn Group, who ran the colliery until it was closed in 1940.

Mardy No. 1 and No. 2 Colliery was once one of 53 collieries in the Rhondda, which at their peak production in 1913, produced nearly 10 million tons of saleable coal. At that time, a trainload of coal containing 500 tons, left the Rhondda every 10 minutes of the working day and more than 40,000 miners were employed in the Rhondda pits at the time.

MARDY COLLIERY. NOS. 1 & 2 PITS.

The first coal was raised in 1877 and in 1888 the two shafts were deepened to the six-feet seam.

This South Wales Miner's Federation check was used on Federation (Union) marches, rallies and speeches and by the Union leaders and was sewn on to the lapel of a jacket. The 'D' on the check was probably for a December march. A different check was used every month to raise Union funds.

Mardy No. 1 and No. 2 Colliery in the 1880s.

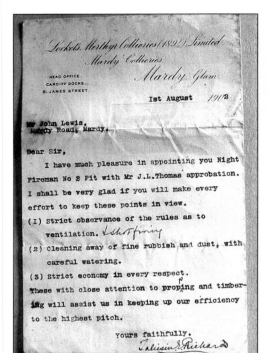

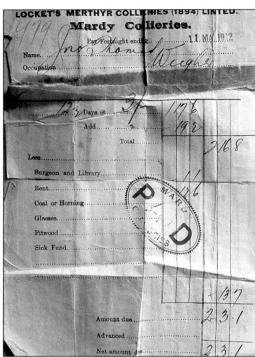

Left: A letter of employment for John Lewis in 1902. *Right:* A wage docket from 1913.

Left: A group of miners taking a break. *Right:* Robert Jones of North Terrace.

Mardy No. 1 and No. 2 Colliery. The building in front was the coal preparation plant (washery) where coal was separated from rock and other foreign material. It was then graded and washed and tipped into the empty wagons below.

The naked flame of a comet lamp like one that caused the explosion at Mardy No. 1 and No. 2 Colliery on 23 December 1885 killing eighty-one men and boys.

ROYAL SOCIETY

FOR

The Protection of Life from Fire,

A.D. 1836.

Patron,

HER MOST GRACIOUS MAJESTY THE QUEEN.

This Testimonial

in addition to a gift of money, is presented to

WILLIAM CLEE

to record his courageous and practical services in saving life at MARDY COLLIERY on the 23rd December, 1885.

At the time of the Explosion (which resulted in the loss of 81 lives) there were 770 men in the pits.

WILLIAM CLEE with the active co-operation of those whose names are appended hereto, was engaged during some hours of dangerous and exhaustive labor in securing the safety of the survivors.

William Thomas,
Mining Engineer.

Llewellyn Pritchard,
Collier.

David Hughes,
Underground Fireman.

Griffith Thomas,
Colliery Manager.

William Lavis,
Mechanic.

Richard Jones,
Hitcher.

Tal. E. Richard,
Surveyor.

David Edwards,
Underground Fireman.

Daniel Thomas,
Collier.

G. W. Cooke — Treasurer

A certificate from the Royal Society for the Protection of Life from Fire. It was awarded to William Clee for helping to secure the safety of the survivors of the explosion.

Mr Robert Jones, of 12 Richard Street, seen here with his family, was a survivor of the No. 1 and No. 2 Colliery explosion in 1885.

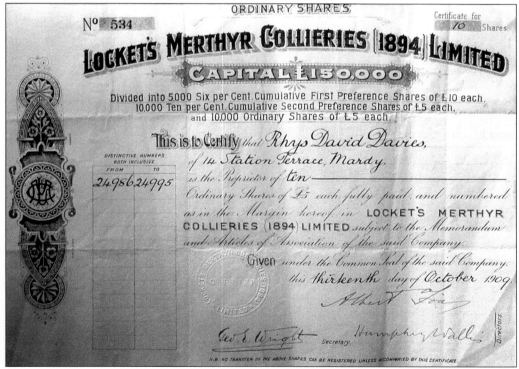

ORDINARY SHARES

No 534

Certificate for 10 Shares

LOCKET'S MERTHYR COLLIERIES (1894) LIMITED

CAPITAL £150,000

Divided into 5,000 Six per Cent. Cumulative First Preference Shares of £10 each, 10,000 Ten per Cent. Cumulative Second Preference Shares of £5 each, and 10,000 Ordinary Shares of £5 each.

This is to Certify that Rhys David Davies, of 14 Station Terrace, Mardy, is the Proprietor of ten Ordinary Shares of £5 each, fully paid, and numbered as in the Margin hereof, in LOCKET'S MERTHYR COLLIERIES (1894) LIMITED subject to the Memorandum and Articles of Association of the said Company.

Given under the Common Seal of the said Company, this thirteenth day of October 1909.

DISTINCTIVE NUMBERS
BOTH INCLUSIVE
FROM 24986
TO 24995

Geo E Wright Secretary Humphrey Wall Directors

N.B NO TRANSFER OF THE ABOVE SHARES CAN BE REGISTERED UNLESS ACCOMPANIED BY THIS CERTIFICATE

A shares certificate on Locket's Merthyr Collieries who leased Mardy No. 1 and No. 2 Colliery in 1878.

Miners 'Baco Box', 1904. Chewing tobacco was usually bought at the Bracchi shop owned by Peter Gambarini. The tobacco was always fresh and ready to chew.

A 'Curling Box' is a curved shaped metal box used to carry coal from the face to the dram.

This safety flame oil lamp belonged to Griffiths Evans who started work at No. 1 and No. 2
Colliery in 1906 when he was twelve years of age. The lamp was used for light and to detect
methane gas.

John Davies, known locally as 'John Landwr', in 1910.

These men are, left to right: David Davies (who was awarded the Military Medal in the First World War), George Davies and Evan John Davies. The photograph was taken in around 1910.

Richard Jones from North Terrace 'Hostler' in the 1920s.

A colliery horse in the 1920s. There were over thirty horses underground at Mardy No. 1 and No. 2 Colliery and their work included supplying the colliers with empty drams and taking the full ones away and to supply drams of pit props and other timber to the coalface and advancing roadways. Horses were also used on the colliery surface for various work including pulling drams of timber and other supplies to the pit head for use underground. Men and horses both suffered and died from the dreaded disease, pneumoconiosis.

A sign on the side of a Mardy locomotive in the 1920s.

This Locket lamp check belonged to Howard Stanway who lives in North Terrace opposite where the old No. 1 and No. 2 Colliery used to be in the 1920s.

Braking a full dram in the 1920s. The drams of coal arrived at the (bank) surface and this surface worker can be seen slowing it down on its way before it was tipped into the washery of the coal preparation plant.

Surface workers in the 1920s. Every surface worker had a skill of his own and these included locomotive drivers, brakesmen, fitters, blacksmiths, hostlers, sawyers, timber loaders, office workers, ambulance and first aid men, winding engine men, bankmen, rope smiths and electricians.

COAL MINING—
(DODGING TRAVELLING TRAMS OF COAL.)

On the right is Mr Maltby, the under manager at Mardy No. 1 and No. 2 Colliery.

Mardy No. 1 and No. 2 Colliery in the 1920s. This view also shows the colliery sidings on the left and part of the vicarage behind the colliery.

Mardy Colliery rescue team was supplied the very latest life saving equipment and were fully trained for any emergency including underground fires and explosions.

MARDY AMBULANCE BRIGADE.

Mardy Ambulance Brigade in the 1920s. The team was fully prepared for any emergency in the colliery or in the surrounding villages.

Mardy Colliery Ambulance Brigade, with Dr S. Glanville Morris Chief Surgeon for the Mardy Collieries and compiler of the first First Aid book. Mardy No. 1 Squad became famous for the holders of the Sir C. Warren's Rhondda Shield, the Glamorgan County Shield and the Provincial White Horse Shield, besides being holder of three champion cups and eight gold and silver medals.

Mardy Colliery Ambulance Brigade winners in the 1920s.

The colliery's blacksmiths in the 1920s.

Mardy No.1 and No. 2 Colliery in the 1920s. The buildings on the left are the fitting shops and the buildings behind each chimney stack are the winding engine houses.

Men and women who worked in the washery of the coal preparation plant in the 1920s.

Pit ponies on their annual holiday in the 1920s. If there was an emergency or a roof fall underground, the most friendly and docile pit ponies would by picked to work, thus forfeiting their holiday.

Mardy No. 1 and No. 2 Colliery in the 1920s. The field on the left at the front was used for grazing and the other fields were full of vegetables.

On the left is Les Jones 'Banksman' in the 1920s. The banksman ensured the safety of the men and materials travelling in the pit shaft. Behind is the pit cage where men and materials would be transported. The cage would raise 1,200 tons of coal over a nine hour period.

The village civil defence team outside the colliery office in 1935.

A rare photograph taken underground in the 1930s of a roadway used to supply timber to colliers and repairers at Mardy No. 1 Colliery.

Ceridwen Street with the colliery in the background in the 1930s.

Mardy Colliery 'loco boys' in the 1930s. They supplied the washery of the coal producton plant with empty wagons and put the full wagons of coal ready for transportation to the dock.

Mardy Colliery powerhouse in the 1930s.

A view from Maerdy station in the 1930s.

Mr Davies worked underground for seventy-three years and by so doing earned himself a place in the *Guinness Book of Records*. He started work at the age of seven and retired at the age of eighty. His record of achievement will never be broken. Left to right, back row: Mary Thomas, Olwen Williams. Sitting: Mrs and Mr David Davies and standing: Miss Glenys Williams (Edwards).

Mr and Mrs Otterley lived at 53 Glanville Terrace. Mr Otterley was banksman at Mardy No. 1 and No. 2 Colliery.

Mardy Colliery engineers sailing to sink collieries in other countries on board the ship *Vitelois* in the 1930s.

Surface workers in the 1930s.

Landscaping the colliery and the tip in October 1992.

The capping of No. 2 shaft in September 1992.

Three

The Village

[handwritten note:] I knew Dr Thomas he used to eat Apple Pie my Grandmother made, he diagnosed me with Measles when I was 5

In the centre of Maerdy, Rhondda, is the square with its old cast iron signpost prominent as a landmark, where miners used to sit and chat, the embossed signs showing '19 miles to Cardiff' and '4½ miles to Aberdare'. If you were to turn left and up through Ceridwen Street you would pass the colliery manager's house and the surgery of Dr Thomas next to the old police station.

Onward once again would take you to the old pay office that was a majestic building sporting bay windows and oak doors. And the block corrugated zinc fencing that surrounded Mardy No. 1 and No. 2 pit, with a large majestic gate on which was a sign written: 'Trespassers will be Prosecuted'.

At the top end of the park, flattened and shaped out of the spoil from the nearby pits, Scotch Pine trees had been planted on the sloping sides growing straight and tall and when dusk fell along the 'Jubilee Walk', as it was called. Below, one could hear the rattling of the old No. 1 and No. 2 pit's washery opposite the old locomotive turntable then across to the river now running clear as no-one walks through the abundant cat-mint that grew alongside. At the end of the lateral railway line, the surplus carriages slowly are rusting through lack of every day use. Grasses and dock flowers encroach onto the silent line, struggling to put down roots into the creosoted sleepers.

Above are the No. 1 and No. 2 pits, and behind Wood Street were the gardens and allotments which were surrounded by green privet hedging and the sports of sycamore sessile oak, holly and myrtle seedlings – dropped there by countless birds. Access to the gardens was by 'kissing gates' of wooden stiles.

Bird life abounded among all this greenery: chaffinches, thrushes, blackbirds, goldfinches to name but a few and the dunnock, the fabled hedge sparrow which crept along the hedgerows like a mouse, very secretive and selective in its choice of nest building. Butterflies galore – the common cabbage whites, red admirals, peacocks and the ever-abundant skippers that flew out of the grass as one walked along, the coppery dust of their wings glistening in the sunlight.

There was no tarmacadam road then, just a well-worn path worn down by the horses housed in the stables of No. 1 and No. 2 pits. Over the brow of the hill a pathway, the 'Lea' which was flooded when the river overflowed. And in the river wild trout used to swim up these little tributaries and breed; there was always shoals of trout fingerlings in this mature hatchery and nursery. The pensive herons used to fly in from the Brecons and have a field day among the abundant fish that were always there.

Reg Sydenham

[handwritten note:] Dr Thomas served the pit when there was a accident

Religious life in Maerdy played an important part in life. Siloa Congregationalists joined their Baptist and Methodist brothers in non-sectarian services at the old Maerdy Farmhouse in 1877. Early in September 1878 the Congregationalists moved to 85 Mardy Road and decided to form themselves into a new cause. Prayer meetings were held at various houses but mainly at the home of Mr Price who, with Mr David Isaac, was the group's chief supporter. Siloa chapel was opened in June 1881 at a cost of £1,500 and on 6 May 1883 the Revd Joseph Henry commenced as minister.

Siloa Sunday school class which was held at Park Lane House Maerdy, 1900. The photograph includes Eos Dar.

GREAT GRANDFATHER
GREAT GRANDMOTHER
JOHN DAVIES

Left: The kitchen staff of Siloa, 1926. *Right:* The wedding of Gordon Williams and Barbara Jones at Siloa chapel, 28 March 1964. Included are Revd Granffrwd Edwards and organist Phillis Mathews.

Parch Joseph Evans. Seion chapel started up in 1876 when a group of Baptists began worshipping at the old Maerdy Farmhouse situated at the northern end of the present Oxford Street and in that year the vestry was built with a membership of sixteen. In 1882 the present chapel was built.

Members of Seion chapel in the early 1900s. On the left at the front is Mr Alf Evans and on the right at the front is Mr Joseph Evans.

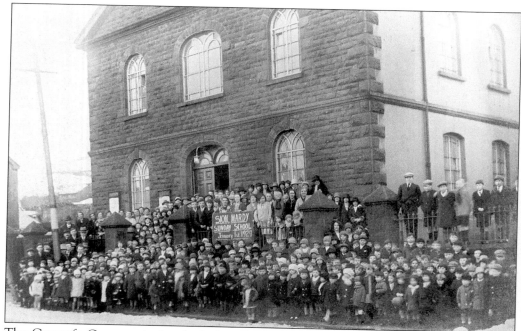

The Gymanfa Ganu, a singing festival at Seion, will be remembered for the beauty of the singing, the *Hwyl* and the family togetherness.

Seion Glee Men, 1938.

Seion Sunday school class in 1943. On the far right is Mr Tom Thomas.

Parch D. Jones at the Bethania chapel, built in 1882. The local Welsh Methodists held their Gymanfa Ganu within a few weeks of the Baptists. The chapels involved were Bethania (Maerdy), Ebenezer (Maerdy) and Penuel (Ferndale). Here again the whole chapel was packed and the singing was a joy to hear.

Left: Bethania chapel organ. *Right:* Bethania Cantata, *c.* 1920.

A Bethania chapel sisterhood outing in 1930.

The wedding of Will and Sal Lewis at Bethania chapel, *c.* 1930.

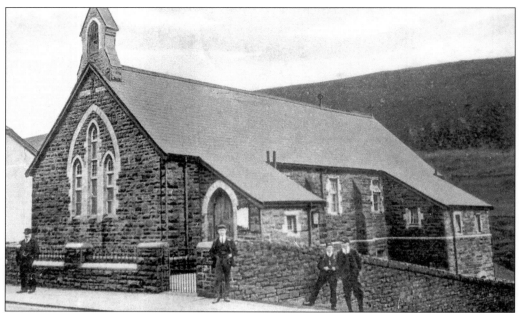

The Revd John Rees held services at the Mardy Coffee Tavern in 1883 for a small Anglican congregation awaiting the building of All Saint's church. On 25 March 1885 a piece of land was leased to the church authorities for a term of ninety-nine years, at a yearly rent of one pound, and on 24 August 1885 the foundation stone was laid for All Saint's church to be built. It was built at an estimated cost of £3,250 with proposed seating for 504, which included: 228 in the nave, 102 in the north aisle, 133 in the south aisle, 7 for the ladies choir, 4 for the clergy and organist. The church was extended in 1922 and the present chancel was built.

This ivory gavel and silver trowel were used to lay the foundation stone on 24 August 1885.

The choirboys brigade, 1908.

The wedding of Edward and Rose Baines (*née* Goee), 1933.

A church drama group in 1935.

Drama in the church hall in April 1939.

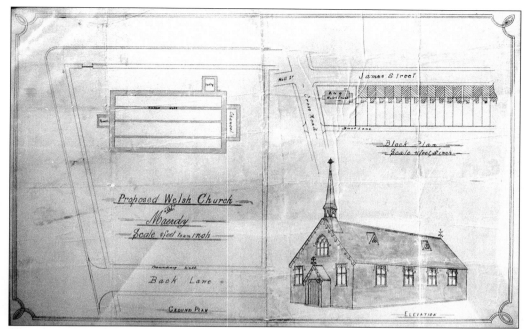

Plans for Saint Luke's Welsh church. It was built for the Welsh Communicant Members in 1888 at a cost of £300 and was made of corrugated iron sheets and was situated at the south end of James Street. The little church always seemed to suffer from nature's elements, the bell and parts of the roof had to be replaced many times and, in 1927, the church was completely destroyed by a dreadful storm. All the items of value were sold and the members moved to All Saint's church. The site was used as allotments for several years and it was said that, 'Instead of finding food for the Spirit, they grew food for the body'. A bungalow named 'Ty'r Eglwys' now occupies the site.

Saint Luke's dialogue party in the 1920s. On the left, back row is Mr Llew Jones and on the right, back row, is Mr Will James.

The wedding of Ted and Tegwen Jones 'Hall' on 3 August 1957. They were married in the Weslyan English Methodist chapel, built in 1896.

Weslyan chapel play school in 1962. The play school was open for children under three.

The wedding of Joe and Eileen Ball on 7 August 1948. They were married at Carmel English Baptist chapel, built in 1896.

Carmel chapel Sunday school in 1960. This church was at one time regularly filled to its capacity. There were many meetings in the week, band of hope for the children and sometimes there would be a practice for the Sunday school anniversary services, in which the children and all age groups would participate, from the very young to the elderly.

Left: Captain Cyril J. Barnes, from a Salvation Army recruitment poster which reads, 'This Army Officer will be pleased to visit the Sick and Dying at any hour, day or night'. *Right:* Maerdy Salvation Army in 1910. On the right, back row is Daniel Davies and on the right at the front is Gwen Davies.

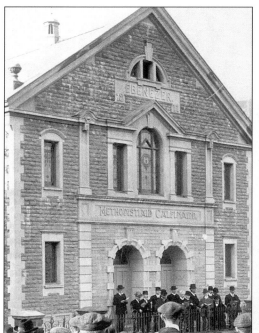 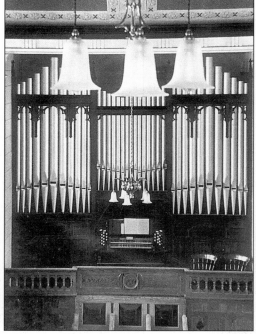

Left: Ebenezer Welsh Methodist chapel was built in 1911 and the opening ceremony took place in 1912. *Right:* Ebenezer chapel organ.

Ebenezer ladies Band of Hope ramble at Castell Nos on 1 July 1921. They include: Nans Humphries, Teifwen Williams, Madge Jones, Mary Jones, Ceinwen Evans, Nellie Humphries, Ann Davies, Elizabeth Williams, Eunice Williams, May Davies, Annie Davies, Gladys Williams.

Ebenezer Band of Hope, 1 July 1921.

The Tabernacle Apostolic church in 1936. In the centre, at the front, is Pastor J. Phillips.

Danygraig (left), sinkers cottages (centre) and the farm (right). The people are waiting for HRH Princess Louise and The Duke of Argyll for the distribution of prizes for the Sir Charles Warren's Ambulance Shield Competition at Maerdy Workmen's Hall.

The opening of Maerdy railway station on 18 June 1889.

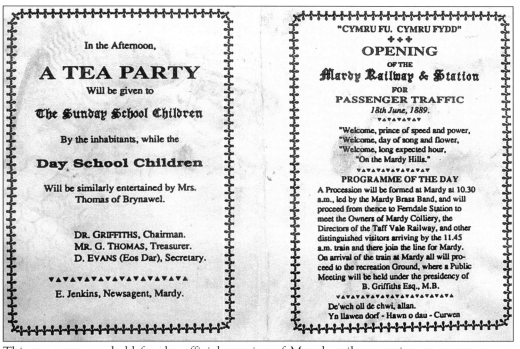

In the Afternoon,

A TEA PARTY

Will be given to

The Sunday School Children

By the inhabitants, while the

Day School Children

Will be similarly entertained by Mrs.
Thomas of Brynawel.

DR. GRIFFITHS, Chairman.
MR. G. THOMAS, Treasurer.
D. EVANS (Eos Dar), Secretary.

▼▲▼▲▼▲▼▲▼▲▼▲▼▲▼▲

E. Jenkins, Newsagent, Mardy.

"CYMRU FU. CYMRU FYDD"
✦✦✦

OPENING

OF THE

Mardy Railway & Station

FOR

PASSENGER TRAFFIC

18th June, 1889.

▼▲▼▲▼▲▼

"Welcome, prince of speed and power,
"Welcome, day of song and flower,
"Welcome, long expected hour,
"On the Mardy Hills."

▼▲▼▲▼▲▼▲▼▲▼

PROGRAMME OF THE DAY

A Procession will be formed at Mardy at 10.30
a.m., led by the Mardy Brass Band, and will
proceed from thence to Ferndale Station to
meet the Owners of Mardy Colliery, the
Directors of the Taff Vale Railway, and other
distinguished visitors arriving by the 11.45
a.m. train and there join the line for Mardy.
On arrival of the train at Mardy all will proceed to the recreation Ground, where a Public
Meeting will be held under the presidency of
B. Griffiths Esq., M.B.

▼▲▼▲▼▲▼▲▼▲▼▲▼▲▼▲▼

De'wch oll de chwi, allan.
Yn llawen dorf - Hawn o dau - Curwen

This tea party was held for the official opening of Maerdy railway station to passengers on 18 June 1889.

Maerdy Conservative Club committee in front of the Royal Hotel, 1896. They are, left to right, back row: Mr J. Wilkins, Mr H. Childs, Mr W. Cook, Mr W.J. Lavis, Mr J. Bramwell (manager). Middle row: Mr T. Leyshon, Mr M. Spriggs (vice chairman), Mr H. Morris (chairman), Dr C. Dall (honorary secretary). Front: Mr I.J. Phillips.

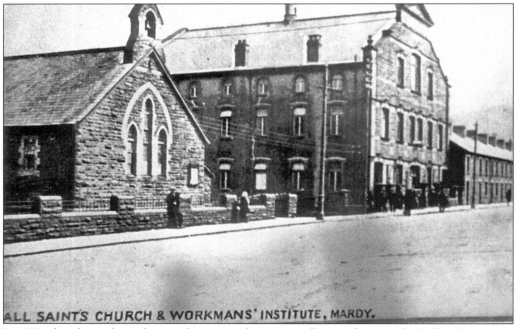

ALL SAINTS CHURCH & WORKMANS' INSTITUTE, MARDY.

In 1881 the place where the people in Maerdy met socially was the Maerdy Coffee Tavern. In 1905 it was replaced by the Workmen's Hall where there was also a cinema committee and a projectionist in the early 1920s.

The first tramcar to Maerdy arrived July 1912.

Outside Maerdy Hotel in 1914. St David Hall occupied the top floor of Maerdy Hotel and was used by the Congregationalists while Siloa was being built. In the 1920s the hotel had six snooker tables and one for special matches downstairs. The hotel was the scene for many events and the Maerdy Home Guard was also formed there in 1940. Available in the bar were cards, droughts, dominoes, skittles and the odd 'singsongs'. The hotel was also a favourite place for the 'Pigeon Boys'.

The peaceful and tranquil Mardy Road before the invention of the internal combustion engine. The first two cars in Maerdy belonged to the doctor and Jack Roberts. Jack's car is still garaged at School Street.

Mardy Square. On the left is Britain's first listed petrol pump which was in use until the 1980s.

The Mardy Electric Light Company in 1920. The company began in 1897.

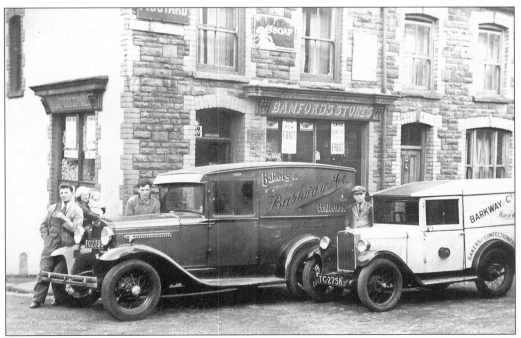

Ready to deliver: Barkway's bakers and confectioners started in 1900 and finally finished in 1960. Banford's Stores bought the shop from Barkway's in 1934.

A class from Maerdy infant's school with Miss Blodwen Lloyd on the left and Miss Bull, the headmistress, on the right. Maerdy infant's school opened on 6 Monday September 1880 and was run by the Ystradyfodwg school board and the first day began at twelve o'clock with a precession from the office of the company to the school. The Hirwaun Brass Band led the way, followed by colliery officials and then the children singing hymns (especially learned for the occasion no doubt). The chairman of the board, Mr Daniel Evans 'Eos Dar', made a speech and declared the school open. The log book states that the children were 'refreshed with a substantial tea.' Then two apples were given to each child by Mrs Thomas, Bryn Awel, Aberdare. The most distinguished visitors were entertained to luncheon at the Maerdy Hotel and a concert was given in the evening. Seventy-eight children were admitted on Tuesday 7 September and on the Thursday Revd W.T. Williams, the Baptist minister, visited.

To begin with the headmaster had to teach monitors first and then they taught the younger children. These older monitors then had to pass a 'pupil teacher examination' each year; later qualified teachers were appointed. In July 1881, at the end of the first year, the inspectors reported that, 'the infants have passed a highly creditable first examination and are well disciplined.'

The Maerdy women nursing class in 1920. They were trained by Dr Morris.

Maerdy elementary school, 1923.

EVIE   GLENYS

Maerdy elementary school in 1931. The teachers are Miss Evans (left) and Miss Morgan (right).

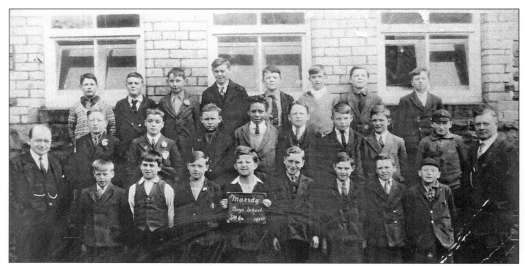

The headmaster of Maerdy elementary school, Mr Williams, is on the left and on the right is John Henry Lewis in 1931.

Children in national costume at 12 Wood Street in 1931. On the far left is Nellie Humphries.

70

Four
Mardy No. 3 and No. 4 Colliery

Onwards then to Mardy pits No. 3 and No. 4. Another landmark – the brick tower chimney of the colliery boilers and the little feeder that fed water to them. This is the home of kestrels and sparrow hawks. The stables on No. 3 pit where there was an abundance of yellow hammers that fed on the chaff from the stables and the opportunist sparrows were always there to swell the wildlife that abounded. The stoat was in evidence, although hard to spot among the weasels, toads, frogs and hedgehogs that proliferated in and among the buildings of the old colliery workings. Rabbits were plentiful, introduced into the area by Llew Walker. The green field below where cattle gleamed fat on the richness of the green grass.

As one walked along the mountain tops one could see where the subsidence caused by the colliery workings formed crevices that revealed bands of peat almost 4 and 5ft thick that made the ground acidic and only the common couch grasses and wimberry bushes thrived in this acid soil.

Reg Sydenham

A lamp check belonging to Maurice John Williams, the colliery manager.

Mardy No. 3 pit was sunk in 1893 at a depth of 500yds and No. 4 was sunk in 1914 at a depth of 428yds by Locket–Merthyr Steam Coal Company. In 1948 plans were made for Mardy to be the first redeveloped colliery in South Wales at a cost of £5 million and would be linked underground with Bwllfa Colliery in the Cynon Valley.

Blue pit bottom in February 1949. Both of these pictures show the colliery before redevelopment.

The screening plant before redevelopment in November 1949.

Building the dam during the redevelopment programme in August 1950. The dam was used to supply the colliery with water for underground dust suppression and for the washery in the coal production plant.

Eimco Bucket 21 on the Blue Horizon in September 1950.

The building of workshops and the compressor house in January 1951.

An aerial view of No. 3 and No. 4 Colliery taken in September 1951.

The two-mile underground breakthrough from Maerdy Rhondda Valley to Bwllfa Cynon Valley was made at 8.30 p.m. on Thursday 8 November 1951. Dai Edgehill bored the holes, Walter Phillips fired the round and the official in charge was Bob Cavalle.

Miners and officials in Bwllfa canteen on the following day, 9 November 1951.

Left: Erecting new headgear at No. 3 pit in December 1952. *Right:* Erecting new headgear No. 4 pit in August 1953.

The office of the manager, D.M. Davies 'the Hooker', in May 1955.

The official opening of Mardy No. 3 and No. 4 Colliery took place on Saturday 28 August 1954 and the ceremony was conducted by A.L. Horner, the general secretary of the NUM. Bwllfa was opened on Saturday 8 January 1955. As a fully modernized unit it worked coal seams at the northern end of the Rhondda Fach and Cwmdare Valley. It has modern pithead baths, surface layout and its own coal preparation plant. At the time of opening Mardy worked an area of three square miles and an annual 2 million tonnes of Mardy top quality dry steam coal flowed into the phurnacite plant at Abercwmboi for domestic smokeless fuel. The depth of the landings at No. 3 pit is Yellow 722ft, Red 978ft and Blue (pit bottom) 1,223ft.

John 'Boxer' Williams (centre), a well-known jolly mining character, is having food with his two young trainees in 1972. They were supplying the G 11 district with steel arches and timber. 'Boxer' cleared a stint of coal and the conveyor belt was on stop all day. The coal was all in the 'gob' (the area where the coal has been exhausted).

Mardy NUM Lodge Committee in 1973. Left to right, back row: Jerry Condon, Will Sly, Brian Vincent, Alan Ivor 'Masum' Jones, Jack Stocks, Tommy Rogers, J. Trebey, John Cox, John Podmore, Dai Bowen, Trevor Roberts, Alan Carter. Front row: Eddie Davies (compensation secretary), Harry Bugg Bwllfa (compensation secretary), Haydn Mathews (secretary), Emlyn Thomas (chairman), John Ivor Jones (dispute agent), Gwylym Evans, Bryn Bailey, Len Jones.

Mardy 'loco boys' in 1974. Left to right: Brian 'Twiggy' Jenkins (driver on Peckett), Dai Stucky (driver and brakeman on Hunslet), Ron Miller (driver and brakeman on Hunslet), Tom Jones (driver on Hunslet).

Mardy NUM Lodge Committee in 1983. Left to right, back row: T. 'Psycho' Williams, T. 'Pasty' John, L. 'Sabw' Price, A. Rossitor. Middle row: A. 'Tubby' Williams, W. Mathews, G. Williams, M. 'Sticky' Williams, G. 'Marigold' Mathews, B. Mazlin. Front row: P. Bence, E. Thomas (compensation secretary), H. Coombs (dispute agent), E. Price (secretary), A. Evans (chairman), L. Jones (treasurer).

Mardy 'Flying Pickets' in January 1985. Between March and April 1984 the miners' strike got underway and not a single man in Mardy broke the strike. On Saint David's Day, 1 March 1985, it was agreed that all miners would return to work and on Tuesday 5 March Mardy miners, families and friends marched proudly back to their colliery.

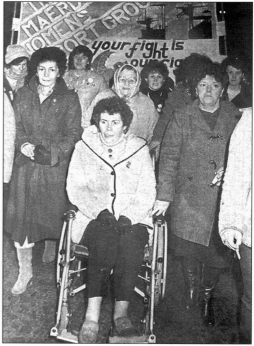

Left: 'The Proud Return' on Tuesday 5 March 1985. There had been fifty-two Mardy miners arrested during the strike. *Right:* 'The Proud Return' on Tuesday 5 March 1985. The Mardy Women's Support Group, always 100 per cent in support of the miners, stayed in existence after the strike to assist with the inevitable hardship.

Alan 'Chippo' Jones with the first of showing of the new work wear. He was the last man to test for methane underground in the Rhondda Valley.

The officials' lodge in the 1980s. Left to right, back row: Jimmy Thomas (firemen), Herbie Reddiford, Don 'Dago' Davies, Roy Williams (Bwllfa), Dennis Morris. Sitting: Derick Thomson (overman), Phill 'The Whip' James (fireman).

Mardy and Bwllfa Boys installed hydraulic chocks at the V 3 Face in record breaking time in 1982.

Left: Paul Robeson Jnr (centre) in 1985. His father became almost a folk hero in the valleys. He responded to the warmth and affection of Welsh hymn singing, taught himself Welsh and made a movie called *Proud Valley*. Thanks to a transatlantic telephone connection to New York he was able to sing and talk to the miners at the 1957 Eisteddfod in Porthcawl. *Right:* Gary Cutland (left), Mike Winder. They were the two last men to ascend a pit in the Rhondda Valley.

Breakthrough underground from Mardy to Tower Colliery on 14 May 1986 and they were only $\frac{1}{2}$ inch out of point! The surveyors are left to right, back row: Martin Evans, Bill Davies, Mel Davies. Front row: Graham James, Tony Shot, Kevin Burke.

Left to right: Ivor England and John 'Bito' Bates.

Ieuan 'Chick' Earland – 'No. 1' (second from the right). He was the last man to knock all the power off in the colliery.

Left: Eric 'K' Kilcoyne, pump packing on the North East Parting Road, Red Horizon, on 28 April 1988. *Right:* Now we're coaling! In 1981 the pit was working the Five Feet at a section between 122 and 133cm. The Gellideg seam at a section of 66cm and the Yard seam at a section of 91cm. The Five Feet and Seven Feet seams were cut by ranging drum shearers, with roof supports on the coalface of the self-advanced types. The Gellideg and Yard seams were cut by Gleithobel plough and roof supports on the coalface were either self-advancing or posts and bars.

Mardy and Tower boys working together as a team.

The last record breaking team in 1990. Sitting in the centre is Dickie Leonard, the team captain.

Mardy NUM Lodge Committee in December 1990. Left to right, back row: N. 'Miff' Smith, L. 'Twin' Smith, M. 'Sticky' Williams, J. 'Chewtch' Evans, S. Eliston, A. 'Tubby' Williams, P. 'Skinny' Harris, J. 'Bito' Bates, G. 'Marigold' Mathews. Front row, sitting: T. 'Psycho' Williams (dispute agent), T. Gazzi (compensation secretary), M. Richards (chairman), E. Price (secretary), G. Williams (treasurer), W. 'Conzila' Mathews (vice-chairman).

The last day – 21 December 1990. Since the beginning of coal production at No. 3 and No. 4 the mine has extracted 12.8 million tonnes of coal and developed 165 miles of underground roadways, equalling the distance from Cardiff to London. The seams worked were the Two Foot Nine, Four Feet, Six Feet, Nine Feet, Bute, Yard, Seven Feet, and Gellideg. In the 1960s the colliery employed nearly 2,000 miners and the siding capacity including No. 1 and No. 2 were 1,164 wagons. The National Power Loading Agreement commenced in 1966 and rest days started in 1968.

Five

Sporting Times

From 'Cattie And Dog' to 'Bull Rag'. Games were played to pass time and cost nothing in the 1920 and '30s. One game was 'Catttie and Dog' – a type of cricket or baseball. An old mandrel handle had about 8 inches cut off the end and was sharpened at both ends to a point. This was called a 'catty'. The longer handle was called the 'dog' and used as a bat. The striker hit the end of the 'cattie'. It would bounce off the floor and he would hit it as far as possible. He got three strikes, and a miss was counted as a strike. Should a fielder catch the 'cattie' before it hit the ground then the striker was out. At the completion of three strikes, the fielder would throw the 'cattie' as near as he could to the base 'dab'. If the 'cattie' landed less then the 'dog' length from the dab, the striker was out. Or, if the fielder hit the dab with the 'cattie' he was out and the next fielder went in.

Scoring was measured by using the dog length between the distance from where the 'cattie' landed to the dab. Each length of the dog was one score or, as in cricket, one run. Any number of players was allowed as long as sides were even. The highest score was the winner. With this game the only peril was a black eye or a broken window. The boys I remember are Donny Lawes, John Henry 'Boogie' Evans, Mal Parcel, Walford 'Sheeps' Jones, Bernard Plant, Roy Thomas, Arthur James, Cyril 'Dabbo' Evans and Will John 'Bonno' Evans.

'Bull Rag' was a simple game played with stones. A smooth flat stone was chosen as a dab and each player would choose a suitable pebble-type stone to throw. One player placed his stone as 'target' on the dab. In turn, each player would try to knock the 'target' from the dab – whoever succeeded would go on to be next target. The player who stayed longest on the dab was the winner. Where the name 'Bull Rag' came from no one seems to know.

Other local games were 'Dash-a-Pipo', 'Hook and Wheel' and picture cards played on window sills. Picture cards were collected from cigarette packets, e. g. Woodbine, Black Cat, Playes and Craven A. We would collect a variety over a period of time by swapping. Sets were built up of footballers, cricketers, aeroplanes, railway engines, Kings and Queens, and film stars, which was educational. 'Marbles' was also a popular game played by most. A well known saying in the village was, "We can play anything from 'cattie' and dog' to 'bull rag'.

Gethin Jones

Mardy cricket team in 1901.

King George shaking hands with the Arsenal team at the FA Cup at Wembley in 1927. On the left in the line is goalkeeper, Dan Lewis, who was from Maerdy.

The teachers of Maerdy elementary school are, left to right, back row: Maer Butch, Daniel Haydn Davies, Mr John Henry Lewis. Front row, sitting: Mr Williams (headmaster), Mr Morgan (teacher).

Maerdy cricket team in 1930.

Maerdy rugby team in the 1934/5 season.

Maerdy rugby team in the 1935/6 season.

Maerdy tennis team in the 1930s. Back row, left to right: W. Stevens, Dyfig Davies Vivian, D.J. Harrison, D. Cohen, L.M. Williams. Front row: John Aeron Lewis, K. Parsell, W.M. Merchant, T. H. Morgan, D. J. Evans.

Jack Richard Lewis having a game of 'Cattie and Dog' in the 1930s.

Maerdy ladies football team in the 1943/4 season.

Maerdy cricket team, 1947/8. Left to right, back row: Alan Jones, Roy Davies, Mal Parcell, Will Thomas, Roy Thomas, Dan Rodgers, Tom Howells, Mervyn Davies, Idris 'Socks' Jones. Front row: Alan Jones, Harry Harries, Ted 'Hall' Jones, John Aeron Lewis (captain), Lambert Weston, Gwyn Davies (wicket keeper), Cyril Parry.

Maerdy junior school football team. On the left is Mr Harold Blake, centre is Mr Will John Griffiths and right is Mr Llew Jarman (headmaster). Centre front is Brian 'Totty' Knight (captain).

Maerdy Royals football team, winners of the Rhondda Ely Cup, in 1959.

Maerdy junior school sports team in 1963. The teachers are, left to right: Miss Irene Thomas (sports teacher), Mr Llew Jarman (headmaster), Mr Harold Blake (sports teacher).

Maerdy junior school football league champions and cup winners, 1965/6. Left to right, back row: Mr Tommy Danials, Mr Arwill Jones (headmaster), Mr Harold Blake, Mr Haydn Jones.

Maerdy junior school sports team in 1965. On the left is Mrs Irene Jones and on the right is Mr Llew Jarman (headmaster) and Mr Harold Blake.

Maerdy junior school football team, 1966/7. On the right is Mr H. Jones.

Left: Dogs have been a keen sport for many centuries and Bill 'Skippy' Morgan has bred many 'Maerdy' bull terrier world champions and all the top bull terriers in the world descended from 'Maerdy'. He has also judged at Cruft's and other major shows throughout the world. *Right:* Helen Gilder and Gill Owen from Maerdy trampoline team. The team was coached by Mr Syd Roberts and was classed the best girl team in Wales wining team and individual awards in the 1960s.

Maerdy Hall 'tug of war' team, *c.* 1970. Left to right on the rope: Emrhys Evans, Tudar Griffiths, Jeff 'The Copper', Pat O'Conner, Brian 'Tinker' Davies, Barry Sullivan, Mervyn Evans, Ieuan 'Chick' Earland. Tony Cheffe is in the 'top hat'. Maerdy won by two pulls to one.

Roy Phillips, Maerdy ABC boxing coach and trainer for Wales, *c.* 1970. In the first boxing show at Maerdy Joe Erskine gave out the trophies. The Welsh schoolboy champion at the time was Gareth Evans. In 1929 Tommy Farr fought Dick Pugh of North Terrace in Maerdy Hall and the result was a draw.

Below Left: Britain's No. 1 Olympic bobsleigh team in 1976. Left to right: Malcolm Lloyd, Graham Sweet, Bill Sweet and Michael 'Jackie' Price, in the bobsleigh. Graham and Bill Sweet came from Maerdy. The sleigh cost £1,400 and the lads would spend up to two hours polishing the runners before each race. As the speed increases on a four-man 'bob' a thin film of water builds up between the ice and the runners and the vehicle is really aqua-planing – a very fast way to travel. *Right:* The Queen Mother shakes hands with Graham Sweet.

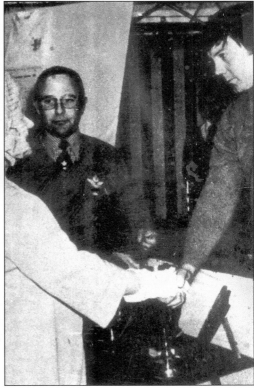

Maerdy bowling club in 1979. Maerdy bowling club was opened in 1916 by Dr Morris who bowled the first wood. In 1976 Gethin Jones, the club secretary, reached the semi-final of the 'Welsh Masters Cup', losing to the World Champion, David Bryant. In 1979 Gethin became the first elected chairman of the Rhondda League to come from Maerdy. In 1984 Arthur Bowen was elected chairman of the Rhondda League and Maerdy won the League Cup. In 1994 the County Under 18s trophy was won by Mark Holland and Gareth Clements was selected as reserve for the Welsh Team Under 25s. A year later Gareth won both the Under 25s and Under 18s.

The comprehensive school, behind Excelsior Terrace Maerdy, was opened in September 1973.

Left: Keith Thomas won a Welsh cricket cap in 1980. *Right:* Dean Gauvain was a Welsh football international in 1987, and was the Rhondda Valley Sportsman of the Year in 1988.

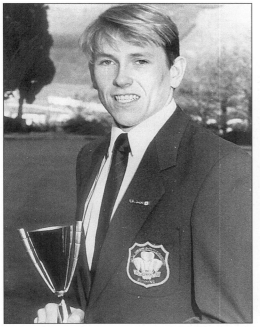

Left: Christopher James was a Welsh international swimmer (1986/7) and Rhondda Valley Sportsman of the Year in 1988. *Right:* Robert Page was Rhondda Valley Junior Sportsman of the Year in 1991. He was the comprehensive's most prolific capped footballing international, achieving nine Under 15 caps and two Under 16.

Maerdy bowling club in May 1997. Back left is Graham Parfitt, the club secretary.

Maerdy junior school gala winners in July 1997. Left to right, back row: Theo Morgan, Kyle Clements, Craig Jones, Lee Marsh, Anthony Riddiford, Adam Thomas, Mathew Evans, Gavin Doyce, Miss Julie Hayes (sports teacher). Front row: Ryan Jones, Amy Day, Nikky Davies, Louise Earland, Melissa Mackie, Sarah Jones, Nadine Pugh, Kile Hanson.

Maerdy ABC in 1997. Left to right, back row: -?- (a visiting player), Mathew Cole, Martin Pugh. Front row: Mel Jones (trainer), Leon Pugh, Gerraint Ellis, Mark Allock, Alan Edwards (trainer). The chairman and founder of the club was Denzil Earland and the doctor was Dr Martin Davies.

Maerdy Under 8s mini rugby team in 1998. Left to right, back row: Adam Howells, Christopher Davies, Nathan Crewe Owen, Michael Melhuish, Harry Allen, Rhys Edwards. Middle row: Kieran Richard, Thomas Williams, Bradley Hughes, Rhys Jones, David Humphries. Front: Mathew Crewe Owen, Ashley Thomas. The team is coached by Gemma Allen and her father Howard Allen.

Maerdy junior school netball team in 1998. Left to right, back row: Miss Julie Hayes (sports teacher), Felicity Jones, Nikki Bashir, Kelly Wells, Katie Hadfield, Danielle Parry, Natalie Evans, Carly Casey. Front row: Natasha Pike, Kayliegh Casey, Rhianne Mace, Jodie Evans, Emily Palmer, Amy Blaney, Zowie Willis.

Maerdy Royals Under 17s in the 1998/9 season. Left to right, back row: G. Woods, R. Davies, C. Pike, A. Griffen, R. Davies, N. Jones, J. Harrison, G. Smith, C. Williams, John Shewell (manager). Front row: P. Pugh (assistant manager), R. Evans, R. Lewis, M. Allcock, D. Pugh, D. Evans, D. Jones, C. Davies, K. Coombes.

Six
Village Life

Beyond the notice of the human inhabitants, the rare 'bog bean' grew in the Maerdy cemetery (where countless sheep could not get at it) and the woody stems of the heather blossomed in a blue haze as the summer ended.

Lower down the valley one would find the ever present 'Bog Gotten' and the 'Cuckoo Pint' that has an attractive orchid-like flower, the bull rushes and ferns were also prolific on the slopes of the valleys. In the dingles and the cwms. Bluebells would grow among the rocks that were covered in a silvery moss that was so attractive to the chaffinch that used it in its nest building. The white pith of the rushes would be used to decorate the bulbous flowers of the cuckoo pint that were pink in colour. The white pith would be wound around this little cluster of flowers and made into a colourful buttonhole, decorated with the moistened end of a match and it was dabbed in to the whiteness of the pith to make pink spots. Bulrush whips and rattles were also made from the plant, which was also used in ways as bedding for sheep and cattle.

Groundsel would make its appearance anywhere and the fertile roots of the nettle would cover any waste ground. The little white florets of the groundsel would also bloom to enhance the view.

What has always intrigued me are the old stone walls that intersected the mountainside showing old boundaries supposedly put there by the monks of Penrhys. Whoever erected these old dry stone walls must have been a hardy breed of men. Here and there in the now unattended crevices of the old walls, creatures had made their homes especially the stoat – brown in summer, white in winter. Stone crop, with its little yellow flowers, would thrive in the dryness of the walls in sheltered places – it was a succulent plant and stored its own moisture.

The flowers of the yellow furze were rare, scattered over the hillsides where it grew in solitary bushes. The blackberry, when left to its devices, would grow in a natural state in any odd place, its creeping tendrils of long prickly thorns would root as soon as it touched the ground; it grew in a tangled mass amongst the grasses – it was a home for many small creatures and its succulent berries food for the resident birds in the wintertime. Most of the visitors – wheatears, pipits, skylarks and the parasitic cuckoo would have left for a warmer climate. The birds themselves were responsible for many odd germination's of the flora – the seeds passing through their digestive systems.

The blue flowers of honesty, the larkspur and the clinging burr seeds of the burdock all helped to complete a natural haven for bird life in the Upper Rhondda Fach Valley of Maerdy.

Reg Sydenham

The first burial, at what is locally known as Maerdy Cemetery, was that of David William Morgan, the son of a collier David Morgan, on 30 May 1877. The minister at the service was Revd E. Hughes. The first sexton was Walter Jones and the houses nearest the cemetery (top left) were the Royal Cottages.

Left: Mr Evan John Davies during the First World War. *Right:* This is 2nd Lt Ernest Sully, of the Shropshire Light Infantry was with 1st Hereford Regiment at Menin on 16 October 1918. He was in charge of a patrol which succeeded in crossing the River Lys and patrolled for a distance of 2,000 yards into Halluin. He captured an enemy machine gun and brought back valuable information.

Left: At 5.30 p.m. on the 14 August 1940 a spitfire was involved in a dogfight over Maerdy. The plane was hit in the radiator, forcing it to crash land in the heather. Sergeant Pilot Ralph 'Tich' Havercroft was found by the local home guard member Ivor Sydenham and was taken safely to Maerdy police station. Ivor and the pilot stayed friends for the rest of their lives. *Right:* On the 17 May 1943 Cullen Morris's aunt was at Mrs Underwood's house in Griffiths Street when a Beaufighter aeroplane flew over, obviously in difficulty. She said, 'I hope that's not my Jackie! He told me just before he went back from leave that he would fly over and take the washing off the line'. Sadly it was true. The plane crashed into the cemetery and twenty-year-old flight sergeant D.J. Underwood was killed along with his fellow airman. They were pulled out by Mr Frank Melhuish, wrapped in their parachutes and taken to the chapel of rest.

Maerdy Home Guard outside St David's Hall, 1940. Back row, left to right: Jack 'Darkie' ?, Ossie Evans, -?-, John 'Shwny' Morris, Vernon Barkway, Mr 'Salvation' Jones, Will John Rossser, Mr Holmes. Front row: Frank Melhuish, Will John Griffiths, Ernie Flooks, Rhys 'Cogman' Jones, Jack Williams (Regular Sgt Major), William Jenkin Jones, James Fred Davies.

Left: Reg Sydenham, soldier 1943. *Right:* Reg Sydenham, writer and cartoonist.

Maerdy's new police station opened on 30 July 1931 and is situated next to All Saint's church. The old police station was built in 1898 and is now a pharmacy.

The police station, built in 1930, is now Maerdy Community Centre which was opened by a group of local residents in 1990. The original building was recently completely refurbished and 1996/7 saw the completion of a new theatre and community hall. The building is once again being extended and the centre is being used by many groups and organizations for both social and educational purposes.

This First World War cannon in Maerdy Park was a great favourite for the children to play on in 1938. Left to right: Dilwyn John and Cyril 'Snipe' Davies. Sadly the cannon was taken away in 1942 for salvage to help the war effort for the Second World War.

Construction work began on Lluest Wen reservoir, seen here, in 1896. It has a capacity of 242 million gallons, covers an area of 1,484 acres and is approximately 64ft deep. In 1969 a potential flooding disaster was averted by a chance incident involving a horse and its rider who, when riding across the dam wall, fell into a large hole just above the water line. It appeared that the whole structure was in a dangerous condition and urgent action was taken. Mr George Thomas MP, Secretary of State for Wales, contacted civil engineers in London who confirmed an emergency and local police began evacuating residents from Station Terrace and Oxford Street, Maerdy and throughout the Rhondda Fach. The resevoir was drained and the necessary repairs made without risk to anyone.

This small 13hp 'loco' could pull 40 tons and was used between No. 3 pit and Lluest Wen reservoir and was lovingly maintained by Ken Mazey. Front left: T.F. Davies. Back right: Amy Davies in 1940.

Maerdy Choral Society in 1947.

St Athan Boy Camp, Gileston, 1949. Left to right, back row: David Millwars, Peter Jones, Bernard Newcomb, Glan Jones, Maldwyn Hill, Ron Evans. Second row from back: John Miles, Islwyn Clements, 'Dixie' Dean, Vince Pugh, John 'Hank' Hanley, Brian Foster. Third row: David Hayward, 'Fatty' Rees, David Morris, John Richards, Glanville Jones, Mr Hughs (PT instructor). Front sitting: Glan Caswell, Billy Addison, David Rhydfen Jones, Brian Goby.

Maerdy Junior Band, 1949.

The WRVS outside Maerdy Workmen's Hall, 1950.

The building of the new Maerdy junior school in 1951. The official opening was on Monday 30 June 1952.

A class from Maerdy junior school. The teachers are, on the left: Mr Llew Jarman and on the right: Miss Hannah Gadd.

Saint David Day at Maerdy junior school in 1958.

Maerdy Choral Society was formed in 1946. They gave performances at London's Royal Festival Hall and were winners at Porthcawl and Llanwrtyd Wells with conductor W.J. Griffiths. Here they are rehearsing with the Cory Band for the *Messiah* in Maerdy Workmen's Hall in 1960.

Maerdy Moss drama group, Eisteddfod winners in 1952.

London rugby trip in 1953. From left to right: Malcolm 'Chick' Chambers, John 'Hank' Hanley, Cyril Agg, John Stokeo. They all aquired the same tattoo on their arms that day: 'Mother'.

Maerdy Juvenile Choir, 1954.

Maerdy Juvenile Choir, 1955.

Maerdy signal box, 1952. Left to right: the foreman, Ivor Davies (painter and glazier), Jack (the carpenter).

Maerdy station in 1958. The station was closed for passengers on 15 June 1964 and the last wagons of coal left on 18 July 1986.

Royal Hotel, Maerdy, was built in the early 1890s. Many games were played including, cards, draughts, dominoes, shove halfpenny, table skittles, and there were singsongs and a skittle alley. The basement was used by cricket and football teams, the outside yard was used for quoits and pitch and toss, the 'Pigeon Boys' were located at the back.

Supporters at Cardiff railway station on their way from Maerdy to Twickenham for a Wales *v.* England rugby match. From left to right: John 'Hank' Hanley, Tudar Griffiths, Bob Cavalle, Tony Cheff, Duncan Davies, Alun Ivor 'Masolm' Jones, Lin 'Artist' Lewis, Tony Comey, Graham Clements, 'Chick' Earland, Alun 'Mousey' Voyle.

Maerdy St John Ambulance Cadets Enrolment Ceremony at All Saint's church in 1963. Front row, centre, is Divisional Officer Selwyn Greene and Superintendent Cullen Morris.

Roberts Coaches was started by John Lewis Roberts in the early 1930s. He used a flatback lorry which had been used for coal and built a coach frame which was lowered on to the back of the lorry. In 1934 he bought his first bus. His garage was in Edward Street and in 1985 he moved to School Street. John Lewis Roberts died in 1954 and the firm was then run by Margaret Hannah Roberts up to 1986 assisted by Billy Fry for the day today running and maintenance. Roberts coaches continues into the new millennium with Robert Reynolds who runs the firm with assistance from his wife Helen and mother Josie.

Building the comprehensive school in 1972. Back, left to right: Dai Jones, Cyril Evans, Larry Satherly, Billy Lewis, Viv Paul, John Miles. Front row: Mike Davies, Brian Evans, Carpenter Idris James, Meirion 'Milky Bar' Thomas, Mr Jones, Eddie Dibbs, Neville Morris.

Castell Nos ROAB 'Buffs' celebrate their hundredth anniversary on 18 December 1999. From left to right, back row: T. Jones, R. Hughes, D. Jones, W. Richardson, A. Coombes, H. Lewis, W. Lewis. Middle row: -?-, Glyn 'Curly' Jones, A. James, B. 'Tinker' Davies, C. Jones, E. Beard, H. Jones, K Evans. Front row: C. Evans, R. Evans, A. Lawes (Grande Minstrel of Great Britain in 1984), N. 'Cwm' Thomas, E. Maltby.

Teify House Keep Fit group was formed on 10 February 1988. From left to right, at the back: Glenys Edwards, Revd I. Thomas. Back row: A. Francis, F. Hand, D. Jones, Revd I. Thomas. Second row: M. Harvard, N. Arther, N. Cooper, L. Allen, G. Venning, M. Williams, D. Ritchings, M. Thomas. Front row: B. Davies, O. Thomas, J. Howells, O Steele, P. Mazey, E. Ball. At the front: Group instructor Pat Jones. The photograph was taken in 1989.

Mr David Hopkins was born in Pentre Road, Maerdy, in May 1906. When the building in Richard Street was completed in 1911 his family moved to No. 4 where he lived for the rest of his life. In 1920, at the age of fourteen, he commenced his apprenticeship as a cobbler with Mr Gibbons who had a shoe shop and repairing business in Ceridwen Street. He worked there until 1930 and then started his own business at 4 Richard Street where he worked until 1996. He gave up work at this time, at the age of ninety, due to failing eyesight. He enjoyed two years retirement and died just before his ninety-second birthday. He was well known and respected by all who knew him and died following a fall at his home. He is greatly missed by many people, he was a 'unique character'.

Alfred Lawes, Standard Bearer for the Crete Veterans, chatting to the Prince of Wales in August 1995.

Maerdy Social Club in 1996, which was opened in 1959. The building had previously been owned by the Co-op and the Boy's Club.

Maerdy ex-servicemen's club flag at half-mast in respect for the death of Princess Diana on 5 September 1997.

Maerdy Conservative Club flag at half-mast in respect for Princess Diana on the same day.

Mrs G. Morgan signs the Book of Condolence at Maerdy Library, 12 September 1997.

Donny Lawes a well-known jolly character of the village who helped many charities. His dying wish was granted when a Jazz Band played *When the Saints go Marching in* at his funeral. Donny was the only miner I saw underground wearing slippers. 'What seemed to me the loneliest place underground was in the Yellow Horizon and that was from Bwllfa Turn to Bwllfa Pit Bottom and from Bwllfa Turn to the Fan House on the far end of the Yellow Main. It was here that an official wrote in his daily report book that he saw a 'Ghost'. Having left the Bwllfa Turn behind me I was quickly walking towards the Fan House with thoughts of 'Lemmey' the ghost in my mind. I opened the air door and I was greeted with a welcome smile from Donny Lawes. He was seated at a desk that he had made, he was reading the Rhondda Leader Newspaper and he had slippers on his feet. His pit boots were at his side and they were shinning brighter than Fred Astaire's Dancing Shoes'.

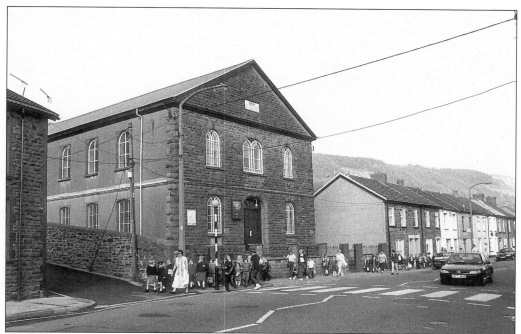

Seion, the only remaining chapel in Maerdy, goes into the millennium with a full range of activities: Sunday services, Monday bible studies, Tuesday mothers and toddlers and 7 to 11 year olds and 11 to 14 year olds Youth Clubs, Wednesday sisterhood and prayer meetings, Thursday night 15s and over Youth Club. The chapel membership is steadily growing in members and has a secure future with the Revd G. John.

Seion harvest service, 10 October 1997.

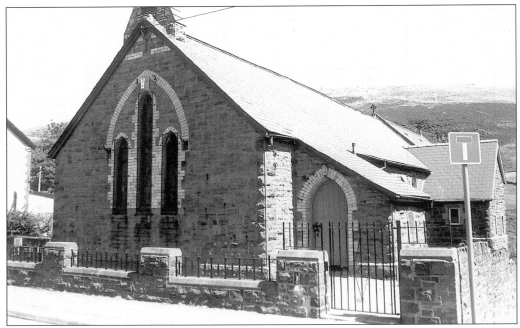

All Saint's church was refurbished and reopened on Sunday 7 November 1997. The church goes forward into the new millennium with Sunday services, Tuesday children's fellowship, Wednesday Mothers Union and a children's Sunday service every month. The church is steadily growing in members and has a secure future with its vicar, Revd E. Davies.

Maerdy junior school choir. The picture includes: Mrs Lynette Pike, Miss Clare Jones, Martyn Dean, Emily Palmer, Joanne Cox, Katie Griffiths, Carly Casey, Nicola Pugh, Katie Hadfield, Mr Peter Blake (headmaster), Danial Parry, Natilie Evans, Jodie Evans, Kelly Wells, Miss Julie Hayes, Charlene Turner, Rachel Pike, Kayliegh Casey, Katie Bromage, Rhianne Thomas, Natalie Thomas, Nikki Bashir, Amy Blaney, Fay Griffiths, Felicity Jones, Scott Jones, Mathew Turner, Teresa Smethurst, Mrs Lynette Jones, Rachel Pugh, Jodie John, Natalie Mitchell, Kayliegh Morgans, Natasha Pike, Charlene Williams, Kayliegh Wilding, Emma Kisby.

Teify House Singers was formed in 1967 and their singing, conducted by Mr Len Morris and accompanied by Mrs Joan Davies FLCM, continues to give pleasure to all ages. Call in on Tuesday evenings to listen or join the singing!

Teify House Guild Christmas carol singing on 12 December 1998. The photograph includes: Peggy Mazey (chair), Glenys Maltby (secretary), Marie Jones (treasurer).

Maerdy infant's school was built in 1880 and the children who attend the school are aged from three to seven years. The classes consist of nursery, reception, year one, mixed year one and two and year two. In 1992 Maerdy infant's school won the Infant category in the National Pan Macmillan School Library Award. The judges were impressed with all aspects of the school's entry and the tremendous use made of this resource by all the children. The school community raised money for books and established the library.

The last Saint David's day of the twentieth century. On the left is Mrs G. Maliphant (headmistress) and on the right is Mrs Mitchell (in national costume).

The Maerdy March

The strains of the melody made popular by the 'Maerdy Jazz Band', lifted up into the clear air above the valley as I stood on the mountain top. I was just a lad, listening to the melodious sounds of the tenor and bass gazzoots harmonizing together, the hair on the back of my neck tingling with excitement at such a gathering. 'What a wonderful sound,' I said to myself. Surely the gods of the Welsh hills would bestow their grace on the sounds of joy as the strains lifted into the clear air above the hills of the valleys.

I walked downwards into the valley, my heart thumped and my feet fell into step with the energetic sounds of the kettledrums. It was wonderful to my ears, but as I crossed into the terraced streets I was brought back to reality. 'I was just a lad with certain expectations before me,' the gaping holes of the pitheads that abounded in the valleys, beckoned me into their depths, waiting for me to choose one or the other and descend into the cavernous darkness below. 'What prospects awaited me?'

The figure of Bacchus, the god of wine, loomed above the door of the local public house; the hazy apparition beckoned to me, its whispers accentuated into loud calls. One thing was certain, if I lost my way I could always drink myself into oblivion and be helped to forget the hardships that I was going to inherit in the Welsh mining valleys.

The thumping sound of the Maerdy Jazz Band suddenly became louder – they were marching through our street, practising for some competition or other; I could see the sweaty foreheads of the men as they passed, their pock marked faces, the blue scars of the coal mines stood out as they swelled with the life-blood of men destined to remain for their lifetime trapped by needs, to earn a living in the terrible bowels of the earth. The sounds of the jazz band faded away into the distance.

I looked around the empty street. My mother suddenly appeared in the doorway of our terraced dwelling; it was Sunday, mother beckoned to me to come into the house, 'Change your clothes' she said. The curt order was enough to stir me into action, so on with the everyday clothes, and I was proud to wear the new pair of hobnail boots that my mother had got me from 'The Dump', as it was called, situated next door to Bob Evan's fruiterer's shop. I had been picked out in school and Mr Williams, the headmaster, had given me a note and my mother had to find half a crown and take me along to 'The Dump'. I had to try on several pairs before I found a pair that fitted me.

I was lucky, I was the youngest of the boys in our family so I always had the boots to myself. As I can now recollect we were a good family and my mother was always cooking something or other and making bread and tending to the needs of the large family we were. I can always remember my father taking care of the large allotments he used to have behind Maerdy infant's school – he was always working in the garden and always telling his boys about self sufficiency. He was quite right of course and he always kept telling me, 'You'll never work down the pit, son!' and I never did.

In the year 1937 my sister's husband had been killed in Spain with the International Brigade. What a waste of a life, and the hardship that followed for my sister to bring up her three young children. My three elder brothers had left the valleys and gone to the Midland to find work – which they did, and I can once again recall that I was about to leave school at fourteen years of age – the time for our elementary education to cease – I had been working since I was twelve years old, earning three shillings per week and the boss used to give me a bag of damaged pears and apples as a bonus. My mother was thankful for the pittance and as a treat I used to buy the *Wizard* or the *Hotspur* comic. It used to cost me one penny for a sketch pad from Lewis the Barber in which I used to copy cartoons of my favourite footballers out of the football Echo. This was a period in my young life when I was to appreciate the Welsh sense of humour.

An example of Welsh humour is reported by Mr Henry John Lewis: 'A person named 'Twm' had been reported killed in this disaster [the 1885 explosion] and it appeared that the relatives of the supposed dead man had come to the mountain from Pentre to claim any insurance money they should receive in the event of his death, but were disappointed because 'Twm' turned up alive and well and henceforth he was known as 'Twm Resurrection'. Such was the humour of the valleys where people could smile in the face of disaster.

Reg Sydenham

Maerdy

Take a peep through the window,
As the road curves from Aberdare,
View the damage that coal can do,
To a valley once fair –
To Maerdy.

This village – this Maerdy – uniquely placed,
This once rural paradise where squirrels once raced,
Away through the tree tops without touching the ground,
Then, alas and alack, those coal seams were found –
In Maerdy.

People came in their hundreds,
From hills, valleys and dales,
The coalfields a magnet,
The coal mines of South Wales,
And many came,
To Maerdy.

The hardships were many, poverty, deprivation and worse –
Workers' exploitation an ever present curse.
The tragedies were many, the mines took their toll –
So many lives were wasted in that driving quest for coal –
In Maerdy.

They worked and laboured in the dark bowels of earth,
And from them came leaders mindful of their worth –
Leaders who fought with sincerity and might,
With passion and grit they marched towards the light –
In Maerdy.

No longer these mounds of colliery waste,
Blacken the hillside's natural face,
No longer one sees the pit's winding gears,
All gone from the surface these past ten years –
From Maerdy.

And now, like a phoenix with wings outspread,
Arising from the site of the colliery now dead,
A large white building lifts its proud head,
Spelling hope for our young, at a time when hope had fled,
From Maerdy.

Mary Howard